You can be a writer!

Teena Raffa-Mulligan

Copyright © 2020 Teena Raffa-Mulligan.

All rights reserved. No part of this publication may be reproduced, distributed or transmitted in any form or by any means, including photocopying, recording, or other electronic or mechanical methods, without the prior written permission of the publisher, except in the case of brief quotations embodied in critical reviews and certain other noncommercial uses permitted by copyright law. For permission requests, write to the publisher, addressed "Attention: Permissions Coordinator," at the address below.

Sea Song Publications
Email: sea-song@bigpond.com
www.seasongpublications.com

Perth /Teena Raffa-Mulligan — First Edition
ISBN Paperback 978-0-6485346-9-3
Cover image: VectorStock
Interior images: Pixabay.com; FreeDigitalPhotos.net; VectorStock

All sorts of people are writers.

Teachers and truckdrivers...doctors and sky divers...mothers, fathers, aunts and uncles...grandparents and greatgrandparents...

Anyone who has a story to tell can be a writer - even YOU.

Writing stories is like having an **adventure**.

The blank page is waiting for a story no one has ever told.

The **journey** can lead **anywhere**...

Writers can ...

Be **anyone**...
Go **anywhere**...
Do **anything**...

in their **imagination** while they are writing their stories.

Every story starts with an **idea**.

Where do you think writers get their ideas for stories?

Writers get their ideas from **anywhere** and **everywhere**. From **inside** themselves...

And from the **world around** them...

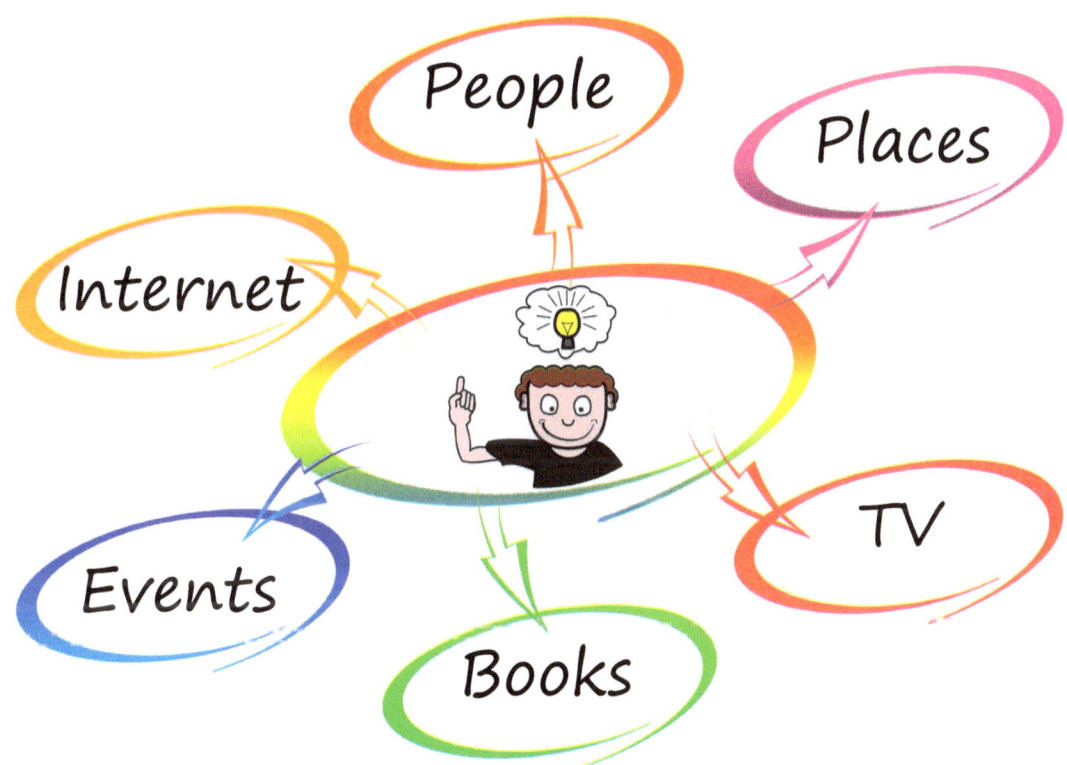

Ideas can come at **any time**...

In the middle of the night...

 While taking a shower...

While bathing the dog...

It is a good idea to **write down** your ideas so you don't forget them.

Most writers keep a **notebook** and **pen** handy.

Ideas are the **seeds** of your **stories**...
You can be a **story gardener** and help them to **grow**.

Questions are like fertiliser and feed your ideas.

Most writers plan their stories.

Who is in your story? These are the characters.
What will happen to them? This is the plot.

Start planning your story...
Who is your main character?

Name.. Age.............

Think of five ways to **describe** your character. What do they **look** like? What sort of **personality** do they have?

1. _____
2. _____
3. _____
4. _____
5. _____

Who else is in your story?

Name.. Age.............

Describe this character. What do they look like? What sort of personality do they have?

1. _____
2. _____
3. _____
4. _____
5. _____

Add one more character...

Name..............................

Hint: They don't have to be human.

Describe this character. What do they **look** like? What sort of **personality** do they have?

1. _____

2. _____

3. _____

4. _____

5. _____

Where do your characters live?

My character lives in a ...

....

Write three things **about** their home ...

1. _____

2. _____

3. _____

When does your story take place?

It can be a long time ago in the **past**...

 now, in the **present**...

or sometime in the **future**.

Write your answer here...

What season is it when your story takes place?

It can be spring... summer... autumn... or winter...

Write your answer here..

Is your story **scary**, funny, **serious**, sad or **happy**?

Now you have some characters.

You know **five things** about each of them.

You know **where** they live.

You know **when** your story takes place.

You know if it will make your readers laugh or feel sad.

Do you have a story?

No! It's not a story yet.

Something has to **happen** in a story.

Your characters need to solve a **problem**.
What do they **want?**

This is where you can really start to have fun.

Ask yourself what could happen to your characters.

Where could they go? What could they do?

Just let your imagination take off.

Imagination is like a muscle.

The more you use it, the stronger it becomes.

Think of **three things** that could **happen** in your story…

1.

2.

3.

Now you're ready to go!

On your mark...

get set...

Writers don't always get a story right the first time they write it.

They keep working on it until it is the best story they can make it.

This might take two tries - or 20.

Keep working on your story until you are happy it is the best it can be.

It's time to be a **story inspector**.

Carefully read through what you have written. Are there spelling mistakes or missing punctuation? Does your story make sense? Have you said what you wanted to say?

Tip: You might need to ask someone else to check your story.

Ta da! it's time to share your story.

Congratulations!

You are a writer.

What will you write next?

Reading will help you become a **better writer**.

Be a bookworm.

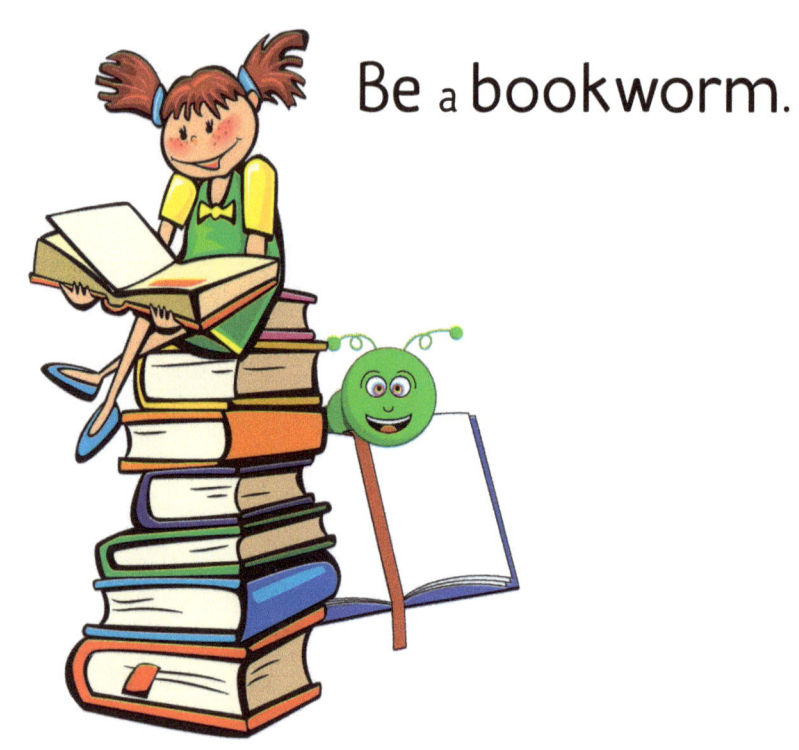

About the author

Teena Raffa-Mulligan looks like a responsible adult. Don't be fooled—it's a disguise. The real Teena is a kid with a sense of adventure who comes out to play when she's writing her stories and explores the wonderland of imagination.

Teena has been having fun with words for as long as she can remember. Her publications include poems, short stories, picture books and novels. She has also worked as a journalist and editor.

Teena loves sharing her excitement about books and writing with people of all ages and encouraging them to write their own stories.

Visit her website at www.teenaraffamulligan.com for information about her books and writing sessions.

www.ingramcontent.com/pod-product-compliance
Lightning Source LLC
Chambersburg PA
CBHW061135010526
44107CB00068B/2948